Handle With Care:
The EQ Learning Journal

Joshua Freedman, Anabel L. Jensen, Ph.D.,
Patricia Freedman, Marsha Rideout, Kate Bedford

Six Seconds EQ Publishing, San Francisco

ISBN 0-9669123-1-X

Published by Six Seconds
316 Seville Way
San Mateo, CA 94402
(650) 685-9885

www.6seconds.org

Six Seconds is a 501(c)3 nonprofit organization building positive relationships in schools, families, and organizations.

Printed in the United States of America

Special Thanks

Since we founded Six Seconds in 1997, we have had the opportunity to work with exceptional teachers, leaders, visionaries, and authors all promoting emotional intelligence. We dedicate this book to you, our colleagues and competitors, friends and allies who work each day to make a brighter world through the wisdom of emotional intelligence. There are hundreds of you who we have met, and thousands more we expect to meet in the coming years.

Some of these EQ practitioners and supporters are: *Harriet Arnold, Sara Armstrong, Neal Ashkanasy, Reuven Bar-On, Connie Blakemore, Mike and Sue Blondell, Harold Bloomfield, Jane Bluestein, Linda Booth Sweeney, Lea Brovidani, Kate Cannon, Karla Carmony, David Caruso, Miwa Chen, Cary Cherniss, Jonathan Cohen, Robert Cooper, Catherine Corrie, Bruce Cryer, Karen Dillon, Joan Duffell, JP Dupreez, Maurice Elias, Rob Emmerling, Peter Evans, Todd Everett, Riet Fiddelaers, Brian Friedlander, Karin Frey, Laura Frey, Daniel G'iladi, Danny Goldstine, Daniel Goleman, Bob Hanson, Aat van der Harst, Steve Hein, Jean Hollands, Lauren Hyman, Susan Kovalik, Susan Krals, Lauren Kucera, Shana Laursen, George Lucas, Ann McCormick, George McCown, Jane McGeehan, Angélica Olvera, Howard Martin, Jack Mayer, Lea Misan, Barbara Muller-Ackerman, Ron Nicodemus, Debra Niehoff, Esther Orioli, Geetu Orme, Charles Patterson, Candace Pert, Barbara Porro, Neil Rankin, Alice Ray, Bob Reese, Milton Reynolds, Michael Rock, Patrick Rushmore, Peter Salovey, Ayman Sawaf, Martin Seligman, Michelle Seligson, Lee Shult, Tom and Lai-Fun Smahon, Masami Sato, Pam Smith, Steve Smuin, Darin Smyth, Jennifer Soloway, Steven Stein, Claude Steiner, Fred Stern, May Stern, Robin Stern, Ellen Stevenson, Nan Summers, Sherry Thornton, Wendy Tobias, Steven Tobias, Fredrik Torberger, Dhyan Vermeulen, Mike Walsh, Tohru Watanabe, Oprah Winfrey, Chuck Wolfe, George Zimmer.* *We know this list is not complete, and there are so many people who should be included – thank you for the gifts you have given to us and to the movement.*

We especially wish to acknowledge and honor Karen McCown – whose vision and wisdom guide our work each day.

- The Six Seconds' Team

Contents

After an explanation of emotional intelligence and our approach, this book is divided into the sections of our EQ Model (see page 5).

Each section has exercises and reflection questions to help you learn the skills and ideas of emotional intelligence. This "course material" is on the left-hand side of each page. On the right is space for you to answer questions, and to reflect.

Quick Start

If you are already familiar with EQ and Six Seconds' model, then jump right into the journal on page nine! If you would like more background, then read the brief introduction, starting with "Why EQ?" on page one.

Why EQ?

What if you could get more of what you wanted, and less of what you didn't want – for free, and it was fun?

Better health. More joy. Closer connections. Stronger leadership. Clearer vision. Greater efficacy. Higher achievement. Increased profit. Expanded personal power. Enhanced self-awareness. Augmented learning. Magnified clarity. Healthier relationships. Finer perception. Greater satisfaction. It all comes from utilizing the power of emotions (see "Researched Benefits of EQ on our website, www.6seconds.org).

How can one set of competencies affect so much of our lives? It's simply that emotional intelligence competencies are central. They are the tools our brains use to define ourselves, to shape the meaning of big ideas like "love," "success," and "happiness." Emotions provide the energy for transformation.

If that's not enough – the great news is that every person has the ability to learn these skills. Some people find some emotional skills easier, some have already developed competency, and most people find this kind of learning exciting. Like all journeys, the first step is to begin – you're only seconds and minutes away from harnessing the power of your full self.

Why a Journal?

In our workshops and classes around the world, people always ask for practical tools to help them practice EQ skills. All the titles in our *Handle With Care* series have addressed that need – and people keep asking for more. "How do I stay focused on my commitment?" "What can help me share these ideas with more people?" "Do you have ideas on making the EQ principles part of my daily life?" Yes! We do – and you are holding it.

Compassionate, deep internal conversation is one of the best ways to build emotional intelligence – a journal is a tool for you to communicate with your most wise and thoughtful self. It will be the conversation of a lifetime.

We've known for decades that regular exercise builds healthy bodies – use this book for regular exercise to strengthen your heart, mind, and spirit.

Instructions

Step one: start reflecting in this journal.

Step two: keep going.

You can use your Handle With Care EQ Learning Journal in any way that works for you. You can skip around, you can go in order. You can write a little every day, or a lot every week. You can use your journal alone, or together with a partner or group. The only requirement is that you exercise your thinking and feeling together.

If you are not a "regular journaling person," then it may be a challenge to consistently write. This is a fun journal, so you may not have that problem. If you anticipate this struggle, here are some strategies:

- Give a friend a copy, and make a pact to call or email every two weeks to check on one another.

- Find a friend who is a great cook, and convince her/him to cook you a fabulous dinner after you've written 20 times. At dinner, tell her/him all about what you've learned. Then reverse roles!

- If you have a "significant other," start a habit of sharing one "tidbit" from your journal each week. It can be incredibly romantic.

- Go someplace special to write – the park, a library, an art museum, riding on a train – so you make a ritual of journaling.

- Write less. There is no requirement that you fill the pages with words! Sketch, doodle, create poems, or jot a few words.

- Write more. Writing leads to writing, so experiment with writing for 30 minutes each and every day – try this either when you first wake up, just before sleep, or at some defined point in the day.

What Is EQ?

Emotional Intelligence is using feelings to create optimal results in your relationships with yourself and others. It is a set of learnable skills, including self-awareness, empathy, optimism, self-direction, and motivation. EQ is an abbreviation for "emotional intelligence" – a play on words because "IQ" stands for "intelligence quotient" (a measure of intellectual intelligence).

Emotional intelligence is not new – rather it is a new structure to integrate many pre-existing areas of research. It is an integrated point of view because it looks at people as whole, complex beings (rather than just looking at one part of a person). In looking at all these ideas and research findings from a combined perspective, we get new insights into people and relationships, into what makes people succeed, and into how to learn to use our strengths.

Real World EQ

You can see the intelligence of emotions at work in your own life. Are there some people who seem to have a deep capacity for getting along with others? Or some who you immediately identify as particularly self-assured or with real strength of character? Look at your own life and list the qualities that make you successful. While some of those items are clearly related to rational thinking, you will see aspects of yourself, including commitment, relationship skills, and vision that go beyond the traditional idea of intelligence.

What EQ qualities do you admire in another person?

Which of these qualities do you have? Where did you learn them?

Science of EQ

Yale researchers Peter Salovey and John "Jack" Mayer have led the way in proving that these skills are more than the sum of their parts. Their research shows that these skills, taken together, form a "construct" that can best be defined as an intelligence – a way of processing and integrating information. They wrote, "Emotional intelligence involves the ability to perceive accurately, appraise, and express emotion; the ability to access and/or generate feelings when they facilitate thought; the ability to understand emotion and emotional knowledge; and the ability to regulate emotions to promote emotional and intellectual growth." (Salovey & Mayer, Emotional Development and Emotional Intelligence, 1997)

In other words, emotional intelligence means using emotions as part of self-awareness, self-management, and self-direction.

Know, Choose, Give

Six Seconds' model for learning and teaching EQ is "Know Yourself," "Choose Yourself," and "Give Yourself."

Know Yourself is increasing self-awareness. It is based on understanding how you function. It requires reflection.

Choose Yourself is building self-management. It focuses on consciously directing your thoughts, feelings, and actions. It requires choice.

Give Yourself is using self-direction. It has to do with using emotional intelligence to build empathy and compassion. It requires sacrifice.

We have identified eight key skills, or fundamentals, of emotional intelligence. They are divided into the three parts of the model. Like all kinds of intelligence, there are developmental aspects to this learning (as we get older, our abilities become more sophisticated and complex). Also our ability to use this intelligence varies situation to situation, day to day.

KNOW YOURSELF:

BUILD EMOTIONAL LITERACY

This EQ fundamental helps us sort out our feelings, name them, and begin to understand their causes and effects. It also helps us understand how emotions function in our brains and bodies, and the interaction of thought, feeling, and action, plus the recognition that we feel/experience multiple emotions simultaneously.

RECOGNIZE PATTERNS

The human brain follows patterns, or neural pathways. Stimulus leads to response, and over time, the response becomes nearly automatic. The pathway becomes a road, the road a highway, and the highway a super expressway – until it requires extraordinary measures to interrupt the automatic process.

Six Seconds' Model

KNOW YOURSELF:

BUILD EMOTIONAL LITERACY

RECOGNIZE PATTERNS

CHOOSE YOURSELF:

APPLY CONSEQUENTIAL THINKING

EVALUATE AND RE-CHOOSE

ENGAGE INTRINSIC MOTIVATION

CHOOSE OPTIMISM

GIVE YOURSELF:

CREATE EMPATHY

COMMIT TO NOBLE GOALS

CHOOSE YOURSELF:

APPLY CONSEQUENTIAL THINKING

Every choice, including ignoring the choice, produces costs and benefits. With practice, we become better able to assess those results and see how one small decision affects the people around us, ourselves, and the future.

EVALUATE AND RE-CHOOSE

Emotions are energy – the challenge is to refine and utilize that energy – to carefully re-choose how we will use that power. Evaluating and re-choosing is simply a process of more consciously directing our thoughts, feelings, and actions, to recognize errors and mistakes, to learn from the lesson, and to make more beneficial and powerful decisions.

ENGAGE INTRINSIC MOTIVATION

People are motivated by a complex blend of influences; ultimately we act because it feels right. There is a big difference between tapping into that core drive and compelling action through force or bribery – "extrinsic" motivations. While "bribe motivation" seems convenient, it doesn't last; the rewards have to get bigger and bigger, and you teach "compliance" rather than initiative. Lasting motivation requires a more complex strategy where people learn to value certain choices and appreciate the internal satisfaction and growth.

CHOOSE OPTIMISM

Optimism validates our long-term motivation because it lets us see the future as positive and worthwhile. Optimism allows us to see beyond the present and feel good about what may happen. It is closely tied to resiliency and to perseverance, which are two skills that most affect our ability to function despite the difficulties of day-to-day life.

Optimists see positive experiences as permanent, personal, and pervasive. If an optimist does well on a test, she'll say, "This will matter for years, I am the one who made this happen, and this will affect many aspects of my life." A pessimist will say, "I won't do well on the next test, it was too easy so everyone did well, and it is only one little subject." The opposite is true of failure or a negative experience. For the optimist the negative experience is short term, occurred through lack of effort, and is isolated. Simply recognizing that there are multiple views for any experience or situation is an important step in building optimism.

GIVE YOURSELF:

CREATE EMPATHY

Empathy is the ability to recognize and respond to other people's emotions. It is connected to optimism because it is through a sense of our connection to others that we see our own efficacy and importance. Together they govern a significant portion of our behavior; they are the gatekeepers of our emotional selves. Once people develop empathy on a conscious level, it becomes self-reinforcing because it answers a deep-seated need to build sustaining relationships with others.

COMMIT TO NOBLE GOALS

Noble goals activate all of the other elements of EQ. Through our missions, our callings, and our acts of human kindness, the commitment to emotional intelligence gains relevance and power. Just as our personal priorities shape our daily choices, our noble goals shape our long-term choices. They give us a sense of direction, they give us a spar to hold in the storm, and they are the compass for our soul. All the "inside" aspects of emotional intelligence change our attitudes; they shape our own lives; they help us become the people we want to be. Our noble goals touch the future.

Know Yourself

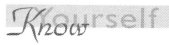

Signs of...

How does emotional intelligence appear in daily life?

Who do you know who has high EQ?	**Who do you know who has low EQ?**

What behaviors show high EQ?	**What behaviors show low EQ?**

Rabbit's clever," said Pooh thoughtfully.

Yes," said Piglet, "Rabbit's clever."

And he has Brain."

Yes," said Piglet, "Rabbit has Brain."

here was a long silence.

I suppose," said Pooh, "that's why he never understands anything."

                - *The House at Pooh Corner*

Scope of Self-Knowledge

How well do you know yourself?

Which do you know better – your body, your spirit, your thoughts, or your feelings?

What helped you learn about yourself in the past?

Who *helped you learn about yourself in the past?*

Dimensions of My Understanding

Fill in each section of the box with your beliefs, values, and attitudes about this statement:

Social skills are learned behaviors critical to success.

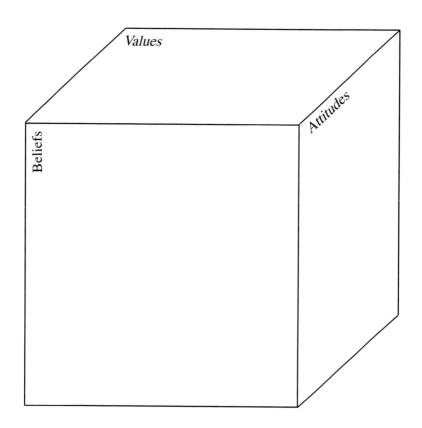

Values are ideas related to importance, or a standard by which ideas are measured.

Beliefs are ideas that you accept as true.

Attitudes are persistent beliefs that create expectation.

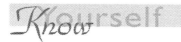

My Truth

You have beliefs about yourself, some seem certain, some are less certain; some you have explored, some you have simply accepted; some are your own, some are projected by others. How do you tell which beliefs are really true, and which beliefs are merely shadows?

You are extraordinarily insightful, courageous, and compassionate – how do you know that about yourself?

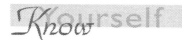

Limbic Brain

In your brain, there is a region called the "limbic ring." Within the limbic ring, emotions are created, you determine what deserves attention, you store memories, and you turn thinking into action. Some researchers say the limbic part of your brain is also 80,000 times as fast as your "thinking" brain.

When you realize these pieces are all in one section of your brain, what does it lead you to think and wonder about yourself?

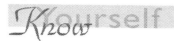

Billions of Neurons

You brain contains billions of neurons, and current research shows there are more neurons growing every day of your life. Each neuron has little "fingers" called "dendrites" that reach out and almost touch dendrites from other cells. Each of these connections is part of thinking, feeling, and remembering.

The are a vast number of these interconnections in each brain – between 100,000,000,000,000 (1E14) and 100,000,000,000,000,000,000,000,000,000, 000,000,000,000,000,000,000,000,000,000,000,000,000,000,000,000,000,000 000,000,000,000,000,000,000,000,000,000,000,000,000,000,000,000,000,000 000,000,000,000,000,000,000,000,000,000,000,000, 000,000,000,000,000,000 (1E200).

If all the cells were used to store the text of phone books, you could store the same quantity of data that is in a tower of phone books that reaches from the earth to the moon.

Knowing how complex and powerful your brain is, what does that lead you to think and wonder about your brain?

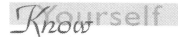

My Brain Is Like...

What is a metaphor for your brain? People used to say that the brain is like a computer that processes information in a series. Now scientists say it is more like a swamp or a jungle where information flows back and forth in a mix. What does that tell you about feeling and thinking?

Draw a picture which reflects how you imagine that your brain processes, stores, and uses information.

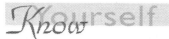

What's In a Feeling?

When you have a feeling, there is a mixture of "thinking" and "emotion" – some feelings involve a lot more thinking (they are "cognitively saturated") while others are more visceral. In any case, there is a "flood" of chemicals that pours through your brain and body, and those molecules last for less than six seconds.

How would you describe a feeling?

A mood?

How would you describe the difference between "sorrow" and "grief"?

What are the costs and benefits of doing all this thinking about feeling?

"Our feelings are our most genuine paths to knowledge."

– Audre Lorde

Picture That Feeling

Which of these pictures conveys a strong feeling for you? Do you perceive that the feeling is part of the picture, or is it part of your own past experience? Which picture is most like you today?

Patterns

If someone calls and asks you to come to dinner tonight, what will be the first thoughts through your head?

Are these thoughts typical for you in this situation? If not, what thoughts are typical?

"Your typical thoughts" are also called "patterns." Brains like patterns, so each of us develops some that we use over and over. You can detect patterns by paying attention to what you tell yourself in a situation. What are your patterns when...

> *Someone gives you a big compliment in public?*

> *You are asked to do a very difficult job in a short time?*

> *A supervisor or "boss" blames you for a mistake that is not totally your fault?*

> *You start out on a task and it is harder than you expected?*

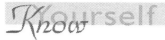

Costs and Benefits

Think of one of your patterns, perhaps one you wrote on page 28. What is the pattern?

What are the costs and benefits? Costs are the "negative effects," and benefits are the "positive effects."

Costs		Benefits	
Rational	*Emotional*	*Emotional*	*Rational*

Some costs and benefits are "real" – they have lasting impact and import, while others are illusory. How can you tell the difference?

Identity

Many people put a quote or line as the "signature" of their email messages. What could you put that would reflect your authentic self?

If you were to design a business card, what elements would you include? Wha would you want people to perceive about you (for example, "This is a classy card, what great taste! S/he must be incredibly smart...")

What are some costs and benefits (both rational and emotional) of having people perceive you that way?

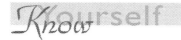

/Memory

We imagine memory as a recording, but it is more like a construction set – the pieces are reassembled each time.

Schacter, 1996:

1. *Memories are constructions made in accordance with present needs, desires, influences, etc.*

2. *Memories are often accompanied by feelings and emotions.*

3. *Memory usually involves the rememberer's awareness of the memory.*

Deffenbacher, 1980; Bothwell, Deffenbacher & Brigham, 1987:

   Confidence that a memory is accurate is not correlated with the accuracy of the memory.

What does this tell you about memory?

About being right?

It is extraordinarily difficult to be uncertain about things when one is certain.

- Robyn Dawes

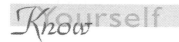

Focus

We always actually focus on only one source at a given time. When it seems like we have a broader focus or appears that we are multi-tasking, we are actually alternating attention back and forth at near the speed of light.

Your hippocampus determines your focus – it activates so you remember, and it is triggered by contrast/change, and by feeling.

Where do you give attention?

Anger

Add to these lists:

PROS AND CONS

provides energy	clogs energy/ drains energy
uncover "hidden" truth	dilutes joy
releases fog of denial	keeps us off track/ in circles
real/indispensable	contributes to retaliation/revenge
contributes to action	maniuplative
creates change	self defeating

_____	_____
_____	_____
_____	_____
_____	_____
_____	_____

Star the one(s) for which you use anger.

"It is better to swallow words than to have to eat them later."

— F.D. Roosevelt

Who Am I?

Describe yourself as if you were a character in a story.

"We are the hero of our own story.""

– Mary McCarthy

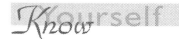

Brain Gender

*Do you believe that men and women think differently? How do you know?
What evidence do you have? To what do you attribute the difference(s)?*

"Sometimes I wonder if men and women suit each other.
Perhaps they should live next door and just visit now and then."

— Katherine Hepburn

EQ Success

What qualities make you successful?

_____   _____

_____   _____

_____   _____

_____   _____

What qualities does/did a mentor or hero of yours demonstrate on a regular basis?

_____   _____

_____   _____

_____   _____

_____   _____

Which of these are a result of emotional intelligence or competence?

How Well Do You Know Yourself?

1) *Are you reflective? How do you express anger - volcanic or repressed? What do you do when anxious or sad - eat, exercise, call a friend, play music?*

2) *Do you pay attention to feedback from others? From yourself?*

3) *How close does your self-description match your mother's, significant other's, HS teacher's, neighbor's, boss's, employee's description of you?*

4) *Do you consider consequences? Do you have a process for making decisions?*

5) *Can you re-choose? Re-evaluate? Change your mind? How? When? Why?*

"*We don't see things as they are; we see things as we are.*"

— Anaïs Nin

Self-Reflection Two

6) *What is your motivation quotient? How do you verify this number? What evidence do you have? Are you more driven by intrinsic or extrinsic rewards?*

7) *How about optimism? How easily do you slide into and stay in depression/anxiety/distress?*

8) *Can you persevere when you meet life's inevitable frustrations, challenges, and setbacks?*

9) *Can you finish the sentence "I feel..." with precise ideas or perceptions?*

10) *Do you act or react? Are you genuine in those actions/reactions?*

"It takes two to speak truth-- one to speak and one to hear."

— Henry David Thoreau

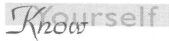

Self-Reflection Three

11) Do people know "the real you?" Do you?

12) How often are your thoughts, feelings, and actions other-directed? How many conscious acts of kindness do you perform daily?

13) Are you committed to making the world a better place?

14) Are you content with your legacy?

"Many a time I have wanted to stop talking and find out what I really believed."

— Walter Lippmann

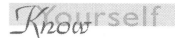

Delaying Gratification

"Delaying gratification" means not doing something right now even though you want to. Can you postpone gratification? Think of something you want badly. Can you put it off 24 hours, 1 month, 6 months, 1 year?

What strategies do you use? Two "standards" are to pretend you do not really want it, or to distract yourself with something else.

"You cannot dream yourself into a character; you must hammer and forge yourself one."

– James A. Froude

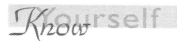

Group Roles

What kinds of roles do you typically play in groups? Are you a rebel, harmonizer, timekeeper, motivator, initiator, loner, outcast, boss, manager, leader, ally, improver, detractor, jokester, or something else?

- *Devil's Advocate — you question assumptions and provoke discussion or conflict — even at the expense of cooperation.*

- *Dogmatizer — you espouse an inflexible set of values which do not allow any compromise.*

- *Expert — you sometimes use your status, career, experience or research as a bludgeon to give your point of view more weight.*

- *Facilitator — you are a "traffic cop" and try to keep the discussion moving forward.*

- *Harmonizer — you want each person's needs to be heard and attempt to balance different points of view.*

- *Jokester — you won't take any part of this seriously, and while you lighten the mood, you go too far.*

- *Manipulator — you have a hidden agenda and use the situation to advance your point of view about another issue.*

- *Mirror — you repeat and clarify what others have said.*

- *Name Caller — you put down others by labeling them.*

- *Pleaser — you want to make every-one happy, and agree even to contradictory ideas.*

- *Pollyanna — you are determined to see the best in every situation and want everyone to be happy with what's happening.*

- *Pontificator — you draw out any idea because you love to talk and think out loud.*

- *Rebel — you are angry, cynical and negative towards everyone and reject even good ideas.*

- *Resister — you avoid coming to any decision and insist on more process.*

- *Shouter — when you don't get what you want, you raise your voice.*

- *Solver — you try to come to compromise or consensus right away.*

- *Time Keeper — you are concerned that people all get to speak and participate.*

- *Wet Blanket — you let your bitterness and negativity suck the life out of the group.*

- *Withdrawer — you protest the activity or punish the group by "loudly" not speaking.*

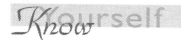

Projection

*"A man never discloses his own character so
clearly as when he describes another's."*

– Jean Paul Richter

*Consider someone who is able to make you totally frustrated – perhaps a
sibling? What does s/he do that makes you so angry?*

Which of these are also your behaviors or attributes?

"Many persons have a wrong idea of what constitutes true happiness. It is not attained through self-gratification but through fidelity to a worthy purpose."

– Helen Keller

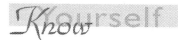
Humor

Can you laugh at yourself?

Think of a time when a light-hearted response broke the ice or relieved the tension in a situation. Was it humor or sarcasm?

Do you use sarcasm? When? Why?

What are the effects of sarcasm? Of non-sarcastic humor?

"Laughter is the sun that drives the winter from the human face."

— Victor Hugo

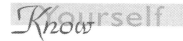

Courage

"Whatever you do, you need courage. Whatever course you decide upon, there is always someone to tell you that you are wrong. There are always difficulties arising that tempt you to believe your critics are right. To map out a course of action and follow it to an end requires some of the same courage that a soldier needs. Peace has its victories, but it takes brave men and women to win them."

– Ralph Waldo Emerson

How courageous are you?

How do you know? What evidence do you have?

If you had more courage, what would that look like?

"There are some things you learn best in calm, and some in storm."

– Willa Cather

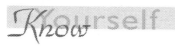
Perseverance

"Press on: nothing in the world can take the place of perseverance. Talent will not; nothing is more common than unsuccessful men with talent. Genius will not; unrewarded genius is almost a proverb. Education will not; the world is full of educated derelicts. Persistence and determination alone are omnipotent."

— *Calvin Coolidge*

"Persevere" means steady persistence, or steadfastness. What does it mean to be steadfast? To what beliefs, behaviors, or people are you steadfast?

Not hammer strokes, but dance of the water sings the pebbles into perfection.

– Rabindranath Tagore

Creativity

One definition of creativity is "Putting together two unrelated ideas in a new way." How do you define it?

There are many kinds of creativity – which are your strengths?

Those who lose dreaming are lost.

– Australian Aboriginal proverb

Patterns Revisited

A pattern is a sequence of thought, feeling, and action that your brain uses to respond to situation. The benefit of patterns is that they are convenient, and comfortable. The cost is that they can lead us to a negative result over and over. Trace the path of a pattern:

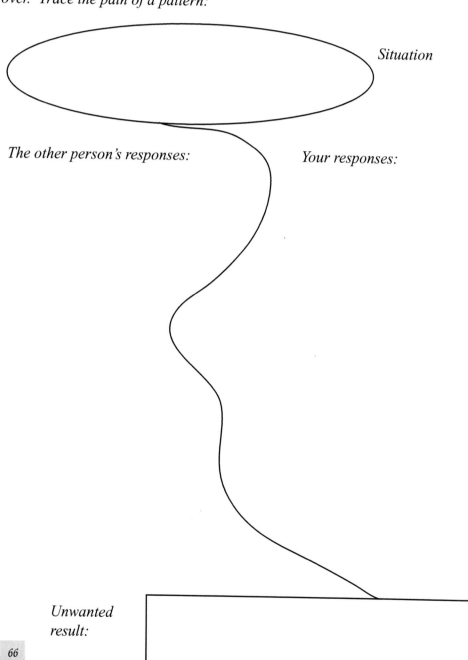

Situation

The other person's responses:

Your responses:

Unwanted result:

habit is habit, and not to be thrown out of the window by any man, but coaxed downstairs on step at a time.

--Mark Twain

EQ Assessment

Rate yourself on a scale from 1-10, where 10 means that you are exceptiona◦ strong in this area. For each, give an example or evidence that shows why you gave that rating:

☐ *I know my patterns*

☐ *I know my fears*

☐ *I know my own feelings*

☐ *I know the difference between grief and sorrow*

☐ *I am perseverant*

☐ *I am courageous*

☐ *I am forgiving*

☐ *I have great value*

☐ *I am a good friend*

☐ *I know my "hot buttons"*

☐ *I trust others appropriately*

☐ *I trust myself*

☐ *I am self-reflective*

☐ *I am optimistic*

☐ *I am self-motivated*

☐ *I have a variety of effective ways of communicating*

☐ *I solve interpersonal problems effectively*

"Any idiot can face a crisis; it is the day to day living that wears you out."

– Anton Chekhov

Emotional Dashboard

What do the indicators on your "emotional dashboard" say right now?

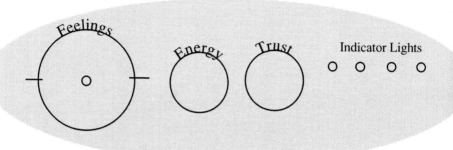

What line from a poem or song represents your commitment to learning and engaging today?

"Life is change. Growth is optional. Choose wisely."

— Karen Kaiser Clark

The real questions are the ones that obtrude upon your consciousness whether you like it or not, the ones that make your mind start vibrating like a jackhammer, the ones that you "come to terms with" only to discover that they are still there. The real questions refuse to be placated. They barge into your life at the times when it seems most important for them to stay away. They are the questions asked most frequently and answered most inadequately, the ones that reveal their true natures slowly, reluctantly, most often against your will.

- Ingrid Bengi.

Choose

Yourself

	Thoughts	Feelings	Actions
Total Choice			
No Choice			

How much choice do you have in your thoughts, feelings, and actions?
Give examples and place them on the continuum from "no choice" to "total choice."

"It's choice - not chance - that determines your destiny."

– Jean Nidetch

Choosing a Label

In one word, how would you like to be known? Just? Compassionate? Smart?

Every day this week, look at this word, and write about the actions you took to make the goal come true.

"I don't believe in failure. It is not failure if your enjoyed the process."

– Oprah Winfrey

Ideal Friend

*List the qualities of your ideal friend. How would s/he act, listen, care? Wha
would s/he do to make you feel special?*

*Which of those qualities are a part of you as a friend? Which do you
demonstrate daily?*

*Do you have friends who help you "be the most that you can be"? How abou
friends who do not?*

List the costs and benefits of these relationships:

Helping Friends		Non-helping Friends	
Costs	Benefits	Costs	Benefits

"Where there is great love there are always miracles."

— Willa Cather

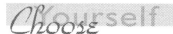

Inquiry

*At the start of each day this week, make a list of three questions that **matter** to you – that are emotionally engaging and meaningful to you. Each day, ask your questions to three difference people. Do the qualities of the conversation and thinking change between and among individuals?*

It is better to ask some of the questions than to know all the answers.

- James Thurber (1894 - 1961)

've your questions now, and perhaps even without knowing it, you
ill live along some distant day into your answers.

- Rainer Maria Rilke

Listening

"Everything has been said before, but since nobody listens we have to keep going back and beginning all over again."

— *Andre Gide, Le traite du Narcisse (1891)*

For one day, just pay attention to the way you do and do not listen. Ask yourself these questions throughout the day:

- am I listening to the words, or what is beyond and beneath the words?

- am I listening only to the beginning, or sticking it out to the end?

- am I listening to find a way to respond, or to get my turn?

- am I listening for myself, or for "us"?

- am I listening with my intellect only? My heart only?

Then, for each day this week, set yourself a daily objective to experiment with doing one thing differently in the way you listen.

"Every person in this life has something to teach me –
and as soon as I accept that, I open myself to truly listening."

- Catherine Doucette

Timing is Everything

Do you know when to select the "best" of these polar opposites? Give an example for each

Hold On. . . . . Let Go _____

Fight . . . . Pull Back _____

Do . . . . Be _____

Jump To it . . . . Sit On It _____

Wait. . . . . Leave _____

Be With Another . . . . Be Alone _____

Pull Weeds. . . . . Pick Figs _____

Speak Up. . . . . Be Silent _____

Hit . . . . Bunt _____

Create . . . . Imitate _____

Set Rules . . . . Follow Rules _____

Transcend Boundaries. . . . . . . Honor Boundaries _____

Resurrect . . . . Disintegrate _____

Give. . . . . Take _____

Anger

Gunpowder has produced great beauty, solved impossible problems, and killed and maimed millions. It is inherently dangerous, but not inherently bad. Likewise, anger is a primal force with capacity for great production or great destruction.

Anger is misunderstood, and often closely tied to feelings of fear, shame, loss, and joy. It feels powerful and righteous, terrifying and dehumanizing, effective and out of control. Contributing to the confusion are volumes of contradictory thinking on anger. Some "schools of thought" advocate raw expression – get it out, hit the pillow, scream and rage 'till it is "out of your system." Meanwhile research indicates that venting is at best gratuitous, and most likely simply increases the potency of the feeling.

On the other hand, shrinking from anger leads to powerlessness and more fear. How often have you heard, "It made me so mad I decided I'd just do something about it... and I did!" The challenge is refining the energy and directing it toward action.

What do you get from anger?

What would you get from "less" anger? From "no" anger?

The process for "refining" anger is simple: Pause, Analyze, Choose, Act. Repeat. Following the process when you are angry is not easy.

How could you use the "refining" process?

You may have a fresh start any moment your choose, for this thing
we call "failure" is not the falling down, but the staying down."

— Mary Pickford

Venting

Psychologists Brad Bushman and Angela Stack of Iowa State University and Roy Baumeister of Case Western Reserve University tested "venting" and found that it increased aggression. Both the study and control groups were insulted by an unseen "peer," then had the opportunity to "punish" him by pressing a button that would provide a painfully loud noise. Before pushing the button, the study group hit a punching bag for 10 minutes to vent, and the other group waited. As a group, the "punchers" pushed the button far longer (Journal of Personality and Social Psychology 1999).

How do you usually express anger? After reading about this study, what might you do differently?

"Fall seven times, stand up eight."

— Japanese proverb

Collaboration

What is the difference between collaboration and cooperation?

What are the costs and benefits of competition? Of collaboration?

Are you typically more inclined to collaboration, cooperation, or competition?

In what situations or contexts are you most effective as a collaborator? What brings that out in you?

Does your brain prefer competition or collaboration? Which makes it most productive?

Competition

Myths	Facts
Humans are naturally competitive.	Competition is cultural (learned).
Competitive games are fun.	In sports, frowns are 10x as common as smiles
Competition creates innovation.	Competition decreases creative solutions.

"Make yourself necessary to somebody."

– Ralph Waldo Emerson

Links in the Chain

What are the steps that lead to each result?

Collaboration

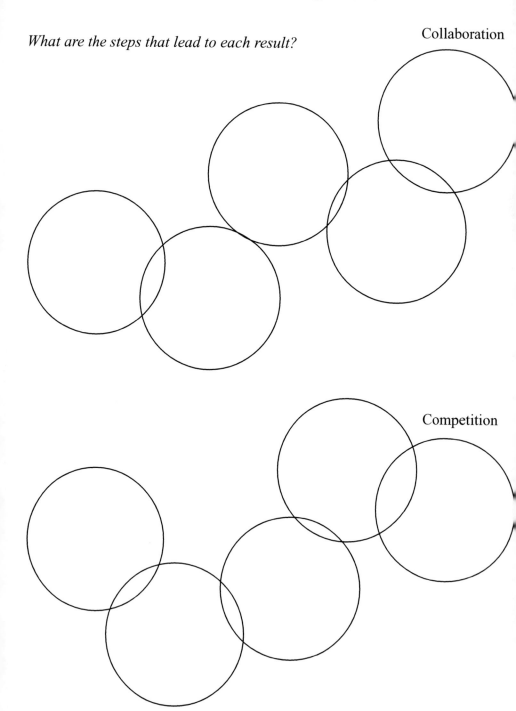

Competition

Which chain is the one in which you most often participate? Why?

"Discretion is the better part of communication."

– Marsha Rideout

Conflict Is...

What are some of the outcomes of conflict?

+

−

"Difficulties are meant to rouse, not discourage.
The human spirit is to grow strong by conflict."
— William Ellery Channing

Transforming Conflict

To get more of the positive outcomes of conflict, and less of the negative outcomes, one key is to change the patterns. Usually when two people have conflict, they fall into the same rut – probably escalating without even meaning to. Which escalators do you usually use?

What de-escalators would you be willing to try? What happens when you experiment with them?

Escalators	*De-escalators*
• accuse	• accept
• aggrandize	• acknowledge
• assume	• adapt
• blackmail	• affirm
• blame	• "change shoes"
• cave-in	• empathize
• demand	• invite
• gloat	• listen
• justify	• modify
• oversimplify	• pause
• placate	• re-phrase
• punish	• recognize need
• ridicule	• share
• turn off	• take responsibility
• ultimatum	• take time
• undermine	• touch
• withdraw	• "we", "us" or "our"

"Always pass a plate of forgiveness before each verbal feast."

– Anabel Jensen

Seeking Solutions

Typically people solve problems by jumping to "what to do" before they have thought through the situation. First, 80% of your time and energy should go to understanding, then 20% to solving.

What is the problem you want to solve?

How well do you understand the problem? If necessary, go back and analyze.

Ask yourself, "Do I want to be right, or do I want to solve the problem?"

Identify three or more options. If you stop at two, you probably are setting up a win/lose situation.

Discovery consists of seeing what everybody has seen and thinking what nobody has thought.

— *Albert von Szent-Gyorgyi*

Trust

"A person who trusts no one can't be trusted."

- Jerome Blattner

On the one hand, trust is earned, on the other it is given. Trust is earned by matching expectations – two people make an agreement, they follow through, and then they recognize trustworthiness in one another. Ironically, we make the people about whom we care earn trust, while we give it freely to strangers – for example, we get on a plane knowing nothing about the pilot.

John Whitney (The Deming Center) says 50% of time wasted at work is due to a lack of trust. Start a list of all the extra work you do because of a lack of trust. To what lengths do you go because you do not trust others? To what lengths do you go because others do not trust you?

"Nobody believes the official spokesman... but everybody trusts an unidentified source."

- Ron Nesen

Building Trust

Often when you distrust someone, s/he distrusts you.

Pick one person who has broken your trust. You know why you do not trust her/him – so now write three reasons why s/he might not trust you.

1.

2.

3.

Write at least one action you could take that would demonstrate that you are trustworthy in that area.

1.

2.

3.

Go to her/him, and say, or write a note that says, "I want to show you that I am trustworthy. I think that in the past I caused you to lose some trust in me by <fill in one reason>. What could I do that would show you that I am trustworthy in this area? For instance, I will start by <fill in one action idea> – once I have done that, I'd like to talk to you and think of another action I could take to build trust between us."

"Trust men and they will be true to you; treat them greatly, and they will show themselves great."

– Ralph Waldo Emerson

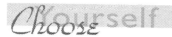

Motivation Myths

Motivation Myths to be dispelled:

1. When students/employees are not working/focused, they are not motivated.

2. Failure is a good motivator.

3. Learning is more important than motivation.

4. Teachers/bosses motivate students/employees.

5. Threats increase motivation.

6. Rewards increase motivation.

7. Learning/achievement/performance automatically improves with increased student/employee motivation.

Motivation is increased by

1. Sense of belonging

2. Choice

3. Appropriate challenge

4. Authentic outcome

5. 360° feedback

"The brain does not need to be motivated any more than the heart needs to be motivated to pump blood."

– Leslie Hart

Trying to Motivate

Suppose extrinsic motivation were on trial for improving achievement. What pro and con arguments would each attorney make?

D.A.

Extrinsic motivation fails to
increase achievement because:

Defense Council

Extrinsic motivation increases
achievement because:

"Intrinsic" motivation is internal – part of your core beliefs and values.
"Extrinsic" motivation is external – driven by rewards and punishments.

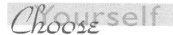

Intrinsic Motivation

Reflections on Intrinsic Motivation

	Motivating Myself	Motivating Others
Today I practiced motivation by:		
The situation was:		
I felt good about:		
It was hard for me to:		
Next time I would/ could:		

Giving Time

Are you tired of always having to "take" time? What would it be like to give time instead?

Experiment with time: enjoy a "stop the clock day." Cover all the clocks/ watches in your house, and give the day to relaxing, chatting, walking, flying kites, etc. Do you feel liberated? When will you do it again?

"The sun is new each day."
  — Heraclitus (ca 500 b.c.)

Optimism

"If you are a pessimist, you are eight times as likely to get depressed, you are less likely to succeed at work, your personal relationships are more likely to break up, and you are likely to have a shorter and more illness-filled life."

— *Martin Seligman*

An optimist sees failure as TIE – temporary, isolated, and due to a lack of effort. See page six for more on optimism, then fill in this chart:

A failure:		
Write both points of view	**PESSIMIST**	**OPTIMIST**
How long will this last?		
How much does it affect?		
What's the cause?		

Optimism is hope with a plan.

— Joshua Freedman

One Small Step

> *"The self is not something ready-made, but something in continuous formation through choice of action."*
>
> *– John Dewey*

Think of a situation where you believe that you experienced failure because of what you are (rather than what you did):

Imagine that you are more powerful, more clear, and more careful. Now, go back to one week before the failure happened, and list ten actions you could have taken that would have changed the outcome:

Pick one of those ten actions that you would be willing to try out this week. What happens?

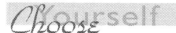

Turn It Around

In looking at a situation or problem, sometimes turning the issue around and identifying some/all of the variables that could be negative is a revealing exercise. Phrase your question in reverse and ask, "Why won't this work? Why is this a bad idea?"

For example, "Why do we want people to be 'demotivated?'"

"What could we do to encourage students to drop out?"

"What could we do to reduce productivity?"

"What are some options for increasing employee turnover?"

As people think over upcoming decisions, potential losses are often given greater weight than potential gains.

— *National Advisory Mental Health Council (NIMH)*

Resiliency

All people experience adversities. Some people are debilitated by them, while others are strengthened by them. Those who are strengthened have a set of skills called "resiliency." What skills are included in resiliency?

Where does someone get resiliency? How does someone develop it?

Where do you get it?

If you are sometimes pessimistic, what is the benefit to you? What are you getting from that thinking that makes it feel good enough to keep going?

"We all know perfectly well what resilience means until we listen to someone else try to define it."

– Dr. George Vaillant, 1993

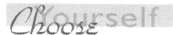

Reframing

The "champion of optimism," Dr. Martin Seligman, says that one key is to stop blindly accepting your own criticism. He says that most people are able to say terrible things to themselves which they just accept at face value.

What are some of the terrible things you say to yourself?

If some other person (maybe someone you like but you know s/he does not have "all the answers") said the "terrible things" to you, how would you respond? How would you debate these points?

"Happiness is a form of courage."
— Holbrook Jackson

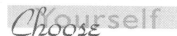

Questions

There are many variations on "inquiry" – a process of asking questions. Good questions are powerful because they engage many parts of the brain. While even low order (factual recall) questions provide important brain stimulation, the wonders occur when we ask "fusion questions" that engage both thinking and feeling:

"What would it mean to you if..."

"How would you decide..."

"When you've been in a situation like that..."

What are among the best questions someone has ever asked you?

Good questions outrank easy answers.

— Paul A. Samuelson

Time

Time Waits for No One!

TO REALIZE THE VALUE OF ONE YEAR: Ask the student who has failed his final exam.

To realize the value of one week: Ask the editor of a weekly newspaper.

To realize the value of one day: Ask the daily wage laborer who has 10 kids to feed.

To realize the value of an hour: Ask the lovers who are waiting to meet.

To realize the value of a second: Ask the person who has survived an accident

To realize the value of a millisecond: Ask the person who has won a silver medal at the Olympics.

– Archbishop Desmond Tutu
Nobel Peace Prize winner, 1984

Do you have time to stick with unproductive patterns?

Where Is Your Energy?

Consider your daily work (which may or may not be a "job"). What is that?

What is most important to you about that daily work? Why, inside, do you do it?

Make a drawing depicting your daily work. What do you do that is most important, and what 10-15 other tasks do you do (thoughts, feelings, and actions)? Where are you spending your energy?

What is one way you could put more of your energy into what is most important to you?

What would be some of the results of that change?

Work is either fun or drudgery. It depends on your attitude. I like fun.

— *Colleen C. Barrett*

127

Evaluating a Choice

Name a habit (it could be a habit of thought, feeling, or action) that you are considering changing:

Consider the costs and benefits of that habit by filling in this chart:

Benefits to me

Benefits to others

Costs to me

Costs to others

What are your conclusions?

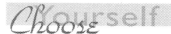

Changing Obstacles

In order for change to succeed, there are obstacles to overcome.

What change are you considering making?

Are you willing to let go of the benefits of the old way? The new way will have different benefits, but you will probably lose the old benefits.

What deep beliefs might be in the way? For example, if I want to make a change to take better care of my physical health, and my mom died of cancer, I might believe that I will die of cancer anyway no matter what I do to improve my health.

Are you clear what you no longer want? Do you see that the costs of the old way are too high – have you made it hard enough for yourself yet?

How important is it to you to grow, and change, and be better? Your ego might prefer you not change because it implies that you have been making a mistake – are you prepared to change anyway?

Does this change feed your ego or support your lifelong goals?

In what ways is this change larger than yourself? Does it benefit others?

"The need for change bulldozed a road down the center of my mind."

– Maya Angelou

Choosing a Change

When people consider making change, they frequently start trying to change before they are certain that they want to make a change.

What do you like/dislike about the way the way things are (in the area you are considering changing)? What is driving the idea of change? You? Your goals? Another person?

What do you have to give up if you make this change?

When you seek to make a change, be clear what you want to stop doing, and what you want to do instead. Are you clear about what you want to change TO? The change-void must be filled with new behaviors or you will return to your old patterns.

Would you be willing to work to make the change? How much effort are your willing to put toward this change?

"The hardest thing to learn in life is which bridge to cross and which bridge to burn."

— David Russell

Change Mechanisms

*To make and sustain change, you will need some structures that support you. "Change mechanisms" are structures that systematically reinforce your desired behaviors – they can be as simple as marking notes on your daily calendar, or as complex as a support group; mechanisms involve **doing**.*

Inspiration for change includes the people, practices, and ideas that give you clarity and energy. On the Venn diagram, list your influences and mechanisms. You may find overlap between the two.

mech·a·nism (mek-enizm) n.

1a. *A machine or mechanical appliance.*

1b. *The arrangement of connected parts in a machine.*

2. *A system of parts that operate or interact like those of a machine: the mechanism of the solar system.*

3. *An instrument or a process, physical or mental, by which something is done or comes into being: "The mechanism of oral learning is largely that of continuous repetition" (T.G.E. Powell).*

4. *A habitual manner of acting to achieve an end.*

5. *Biology. The involuntary and consistent response of an organism to a given stimulus.*

6. *Psychology. A usually unconscious mental and emotional pattern that shapes behavior in a given situation or environment: a defense mechanism.*

7. *The sequence of steps in a chemical reaction.*

8. *Philosophy. The doctrine that all natural phenomena are explicable by material causes and mechanical principles.*

The American Heritage® Dictionary

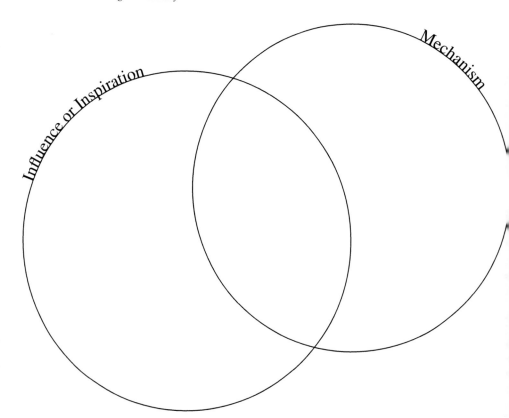

"To change one's life, start immediately, do it flamboyantly, no exceptions."

– William James

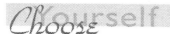

Giving Attention

Optimizing relationships requires careful attention to the ways you use your attention. At different times, different kinds of attention are most appropriate.

You can look at your focus as "time out" or "time in" – and growing and changing require both.

What do you do to create both of these in your relationships?

Time Out	Time In
releasing	listening
reducing	skill teaching
reframing	building understanding
cooling off	supporting

For Whom?

Are you acting for yourself and your goals, or are you acting in response to expectations and "programming" of others?

What is the benefit of following others' expectations? The costs?

How do you know if a decision or action is based on your own beliefs and goals? Can you know? Does it matter to you?

How do you evaluate your actions and decisions – who will decide if it was "good enough" or even "excellent?" What does it mean to do your best?

"*The ultimate measure of a man is not where he stands in moment of comfort and convenience, but where he stands at times of challenge and controversy.*"

— *Martin Luther King Jr.*

"The moment we begin to

fear the opinions of others and hesitate to tell the truth that is in us,

and from motives of policy are silent when we should speak,

the divine floods of light and life no longer flow into our souls."

– Elizabeth Cady Stanton, 1890

Life Is...

"Life is like the Olympic Games: a few strain their muscles to carry off a prize; others sell trinkets to the crowd for a profit; some just come to look and see how everything is done." – Pythagoras

"Life is like playing a violin in public and learning the instrument as one plays." – Samuel Butler

"Life is a bowl of cherries." – Anonymous

"Life is a bowl of pits." – Rodney Dangerfield

What do you say?

Life is...

What does your answer tell you about who you are? Your goals? Expectations? Hopes? Fears?

Suppose a friend tells you that "life is to get yours while you can, and forget the rest!" What would your response be? Would you try to change his/her mind? How? Why?

"One thing I know: the only ones among you who will be really happy are those who will have sought and found how to serve."

– Albert Schweitzer

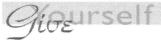
Exploring Empathy

What does "empathy" mean?

Why is empathy necessary?

Who in history has demonstrated empathy?

What person who you know, or character from a book/movie/show, is highly empathic?

What are the costs and benefits of increasing empathy?

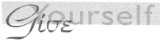

Empathy In Action

How does someone show empathy?

How do I show empathy?

When would showing more empathy be beneficial?

What are some strategies I could use to be more empathic?

Empathy Aerobics

What might I need?

Write answers to the following:

    1. if my spouse of 50 years died?

    2. if my child were terminally ill?

    3. if my spouse of 10 years divorced me?

    4. if I recently lost my job?

    5. if I didn't get the promotion?

    6. if I'm the single parent of three?

    7. if I just moved in next door?

    8. if I'm the new teacher on the block?

    9. if I'm agonizing over a dilemma?

    10. if I were just scolded by my teacher/boss?

    11. if I just lost a non-valuable but sentimental piece of jewelry?

"*Do not free a camel of his hump; you may be freeing him from being a camel.*"

– G.K. Chesterton

s onds* at the top right.

Empathy Quiz

Distribution of Resources: on a scale of 1-10 how much do you agree that resources should be distributed solely on the basis of need? Ask questions to encourage differentiation between wants and needs and who determines validity of need.

1-10:

Rationale:

What do you think your answer reveals about your empathy quotient?

150

"It is good to have an end to journey towards; but it is the journey that matters in the end."

— Ursula K. Le Guin

Decision Making

Have you ever made a decision that was entirely your own?

How do you know which are "big decisions" and which are "small decisions"?

When you have made the best decisions in your life, what help did you have (such as feelings, questions, people, things, places, space, etc.)?

"What matters most is that we learn from living."

– Doris Lessing

Emotional Algebra

Decisions with Emotional Algebra

1. Identify the problem or dilemma.

2. List the pros and cons for each "side" including both thinking and feeling.

3. Give each pro and con a weighted value from 1-10.

4. Design a graph within the circle which illustrates the power of each column.

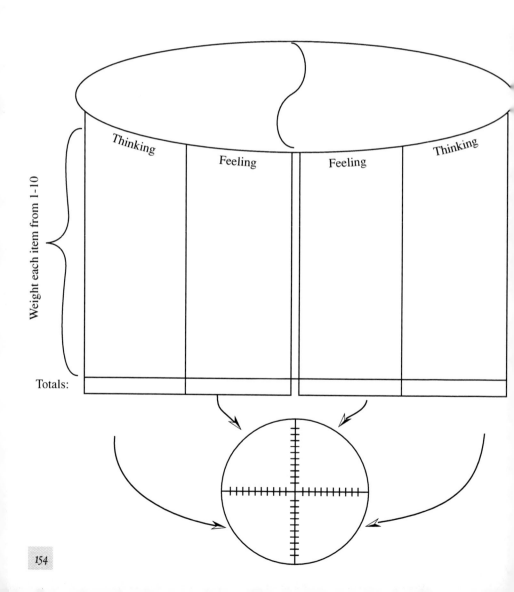

"Behold the turtle. He only makes progress when he sticks his neck out."

— James Bryant Conant

Where Does Accountability Live?

It starts with a belief that "The buck stops here" – that you have the right and responsibility to act. Describe how someone with that belief would act:

	The Buck Stops Here!	**Pass the Buck**
What does it look like?	Bystander helps out...	Bystander walks by...
What's your history?		
What would encourage this?	"Can do"; break task down to manageable steps; ask questions that let people see their responsibility...	Make tasks over-complex; micro-manage; external motivation...

"No man was ever wise by chance."

— Seneca

$\mathcal{P}$ower

Power is an enticing seducer. It tempts and beckons — hinting that only goodness will be the result. In reality it says, "my 'noble goal' is more noble than yours." And usually it negates individual choice — eliminating control over tiny freedoms (selecting a flavor of ice cream) to all-encompassing freedoms (choosing to follow a political system or religion). Held in one hand it becomes tyranny; shared with other hands, it becomes community.

When you think of power, what do you think?

In what ways are you powerful? Not powerful?

If you were unbelievably powerful, what would that look like? How would you know?

"Power is the ability to do good things for others."

— Brooke Astor

Do No Harm

Would it be possible for a person to be "perfectly good" and yet cause harm to innocent people? Could a person be wicked even if s/he never caused any harm at all?

Goals and Objectives

A goal is the destination, an objective is the transportation.

A goal lights up the sky, an objective lights your desk.

A goal is a fancy, an objective is a plan.

A goal is:

An objective is:

From Intention to Action

Turning big ideas into action steps is a challenge. Suppose you have a goal, such as, "be a great parent." How do you turn that into action?

What is one of your "big goals"?

Describe one result of that goal – what is one thing you would see if you met the goal? This "what you would see" result might be called a "milestone" which is a measuring point along the way to the goal.

What are some of the obstacles for getting from here to the milestone?

What is one action that you can take today or tomorrow to move you past one obstacle?

"To be freed from the belief that 'there is no freedom' is indeed to be free."

— *Buber*

Plan SMART

The purpose of setting objectives is that they help you move toward a goal. They can not do that unless they are SMART objectives:

   S = simple (is there only one part?)

   M = measurable (at the end, can you see that it is done?)

   A = actionable (can you take action on this?)

   R = reasonable (are you likely to actually do this?)

   T = timely (how often and how long will you work on this? By when will it be accomplished?)

Set an objective:

Test it:

   S =

   M =

   A =

   R =

   T =

Human Being

A noble goal is a lifetime mission that leads you onward to fulfill your greate human potential. Karen Stone McCown, author of Self-Science and Chairme of Six Seconds, has set "to support myself and others to become human beings" as her noble goal. Clearly Self-Science is one of the results of that commitment. To illustrate this concept, make two lists titled "human having and "human being." First try identifying the attributes for yourself; then, wi a partner or group, list additional words for each column:

Human Having	Human Being

"After the verb 'to love,' 'to help' is the most beautiful verb in the world."

— Bertha von Suttner

Finding a Noble Goal

Brainstorm a list of "never never agains" that you do not want to see in the world, and to which you will not contribute. Your noble goal will be a compass to help you see if you are moving toward these:

Noble goals are:
- *Outer directed*
- *Not finished in your lifetime*
- *Encompassing and integrating all aspects of your life (balance)*
- *Enough to get you out of bed when that is all you have.*

What will you include in your noble goal?

"*The greatest despair is to not become the person you were meant to be.*"

— *Kierkegaard*

What's A Rebel?

The definition of a rebel (according to the American Heritage Dictionary) is
   1) *to refuse allegiance to and oppose by force an established governme or ruling authority;*
   2) *to resist or defy an authority or a generally accepted convention; an.*
   3) *to feel or express strong unwillingness or repugnance.*

How would you define "a rebel with a cause?"

In concluding a mini-survey with several friends, it was amazing to discover how hard it was to answer the following;

"Name two of your favorite 'rebels with a cause.'" Here were some of the responses:

   Mahatma Gandhi, Albert Schweitzer, Jimmy Hendrix, Bob Marley, Carl Rogers, John Adams, Brigham Young, Susan B. Anthony, Ralph Nader, Billie Jean King.

Who would you name?

"You might as well fall flat on your face as lean over too far backwards."

– James Thurbur

Rebels Need...

The battle for human rights never ends. It has to be fought again and again to preserve freedom and justice, and to prevent ignorance and selfishness. History isn't over yet. Principled rebels need to be encouraged, supported, and nurtured in order to blossom and grow.

Rebels with a cause need:

1. *Willingness to risk – both physically and emotionally*
2. *Courage in the face of huge fears*
3. *Intrinsic motivation because rewards are not evident*
4. *Willingness to deal with continuous rejection*
5. *Persuasive communication skills*
6. *Optimism combined with perseverance and resiliency*
7. *To question authority and traditions*
8. *To practice consequential thinking*
9. *Strategic planning to compensate for weaknesses*
10. *EQ skills to develop networks of support*

Which of these do you have? Which do you share?

Are you mentoring a "rebel with a cause"? Or maybe a rebel without a cause? Who? Why?

"Only dead fish swim with the stream."

— *Unknown*

Staying Engaged

U.S. working population is:

26% engaged (loyal and productive),

55% not engaged (just putting in time), and

19% actively disengaged (unhappy and spreading their discontent).

– Marcus Buckingham

Where are you? Why?

What does it mean to be "engaged" in your work?

How do you bring your whole self to your work, to your family, to your daily life?

"You miss 100% of the shots you never take."

— Wayne Gretzky

Intention

We tend to judge ourselves based on our intentions (even when our actions do not follow suit), while we judge others on their actions (and ignore their intentions).

What are the costs and benefits of this pattern?

How does this affect your noble goal?

"The more one judges, the less one loves."

— Honóre de Balzac

Simple Gifts

If you could give your parent(s) a non-material gift, what would you give? What would that mean to them and to you?

"Always be a little kinder that necessary."

— James M. Barrie

Thank Me

What are the ten greatest gifts you give yourself?

I am grateful to myself for...

"A compliment is a gift, not to be thrown away carelessly, unless you want to hurt the giver."

— Eleanor Hamilton

Relationship Results

The *"four horsemen"* of successful relationships
  1. Praise / Affirmation
  2. Respect
  3. Vulnerability / Openness
  4. Listening / Responsiveness

The *"four horsemen"* that destroy relationships
  1. Criticism
  2. Contempt
  3. Defensiveness
  4. Stone-walling

Which of these are your patterns? Which do you use and when?

"*The ultimate test of a relationship is to disagree but hold hands.*"

-- *Alexander Penney*

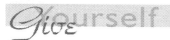

Role Modeling

Watchers do 30% of what we say and 70% of what we do.

Every person is a role model. Who is watching you, and what are they learning?

"The sun, with all those planets revolving around it and dependent on it, can still ripen a bunch of grapes as if it had nothing else in the universe to do."

— Galileo Galilei

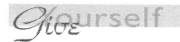

Being Right

No two people see the external world in exactly the same way.

To every person a thing is what he thinks it is – in other words, not a thing, but a think.

– Penelope Fitzgerald

What are the costs and benefits of being right?

When you make yourself right, do you make others wrong? What other choices do you have?

"Begin somewhere; you cannot build a reputation on what you intend to do."

— Liz Smith

Dreamers of Dreams

"We are the music makers,

We are the dreamers of dreams,

Wandering by lone sea-breakers,

And sitting by desolate streams –

World-losers and world-forsakers,

On whom the pale moon gleams:

We are the movers and shakers

Of the world forever, it seems."

– Arthur William Edgar O'Shaughnessy

Does this poem talk about you? The you of your daily life, or an exceptional you who comes forward at special moments?

"It is difficult to say what is impossible, for the dream of yesterday is the hope of today and the reality of tomorrow."

– Robert H. Goddard

Quotable You

Throughout this journal there are quotes which capture some essence of the author. Create your "quotable quote" – what will it show?

What is your quote?

Beginning Again

Give yourself a day to peruse this journal. Read through your entries, and consider what you have learned. How have you changed and grown since you began?

If you were to start over, what would be different, what would be the same?

What are the three most important lessons you've learned reviewing your journal?

What are some next steps? Will you continue your EQ journey? How? Where? When? Why? The next several pages are blank so you can reflect on these questions and write your own conclusions.

"To think is easy. To act is difficult. To act as one thinks is the most difficult of all."

— J. W. von Goethe

"Wisdom is the reward you get for a lifetime of listening when you'd have preferred to talk."

— Doug Larson

Emotional Intelligence Network

Six Seconds is a nonprofit organization building positive and productive relationships through emotional intelligence. The organization supports practitioners and change agents around the world who are implementing EQ projects in schools, businesses, communities, and families. Our team also assists schools to create an optimal learning environment by infusing emotional intelligence in the curriculum and throughout the school culture.

To learn more about EQ and Six Seconds, visit us online:

www.6seconds.org

or contact us today:

Phone: (650) 685-9885

Toll Free: (877) EQ-TODAY (378-6329)

Fax: (650) 685-9880

Email: staff@6seconds.org